GENE ___ ___NAL
CURSES *from the*
COURTS OF HEAVEN

Destiny Image Books by Robert Henderson

Breaking GENERATIONAL CURSES *from the* COURTS OF HEAVEN

Annulling Demonic Covenants in Your Bloodline

ROBERT HENDERSON

DESTINY IMAGE® PUBLISHERS, INC.
P.O. Box 310, Shippensburg, PA 17257-0310
"Publishing cutting-edge prophetic resources to supernaturally empower the body of Christ"

This book and all other Destiny Image and Destiny Image Fiction books are available at Christian bookstores and distributors worldwide.

For more information on foreign distributors, call 717-532-3040.

Reach us on the Internet: www.destinyimage.com.

ISBN 13 TP: 978-0-7684-7466-4

ISBN 13 eBook: 978-0-7684-7467-1

For Worldwide Distribution, Printed in the U.S.A.

3 4 5 6 7 8 / 27 26 25 24 23

CONTENTS

INTRODUCTION

When the subject of curses comes up, there are varying streams of thought. There are those who immediately picture a scene from a movie. A witch or warlock is seen placing a curse on someone through an incantation. This curse can turn their victims into another species, like in *Beauty and the Beast*. In that story, the different servants of the house along with the master fall under the spell of evil. This cannot be broken off until the beast and the beauty come together in a union. As this occurs, all those who have been transformed into different items in the house are freed to return to their original state. There are many good parallels that we can draw from this. Curses do, in fact, alter God's original plan. However, to limit curses to what we see in a movie or television production is an error. Entertainment demonstrates curses to us, but it over-dramatizes their operation.

Another perspective sometimes held by people is that curses once existed but they have no power over us as New Testament believers. We have been told that when we were born again, the curses of the law were lifted from our lives. This is actually a biblical truth. Galatians 3:13 clearly shows that the work of Jesus on the cross *legally* broke the power of curses against us.

> *Christ has redeemed us from the curse of the law, having become a curse for us (for it is written, "Cursed is everyone who hangs on a tree").*

Jesus legally took the penalty of every curse spoken against us by the law. These curses are spoken about in Deuteronomy 28:15.

> *But it shall come to pass, if you do not obey the voice of the Lord your God, to observe*

carefully all His commandments and His statutes which I command you today, that all these curses will come upon you and overtake you.

The curses are then listed specifically. They range from mental illness to financial ruin to health issues to premature death and family demise. These are just some of the terrible things that these curses bring as a result of people not obeying the voice of the Lord. The problem is that all of us have broken the law and word of the Lord. We are told in Romans 3:10-12 that there is no one who is righteous. By the standard of God, everyone is worthy to be cursed!

As it is written: "There is none righteous, no, not one; there is none who understands; there is none who seeks after God. They have all turned aside; they have together become unprofitable; there is none who does good, no, not one."

But Jesus has become righteousness for us. Part of His atoning work was to make us the *righteousness of God.* Second Corinthians 5:21 actually declares that He became our sin that we might be His righteousness.

> *For He made Him who knew no sin to be sin for us, that we might become the righteousness of God in Him.*

This position in the spirit world frees us from the curses of the law that the devil wants to claim the legal right to visit us with. On the basis of this, there are those who contend that curses have no power over us as New Testament believers. We have been delivered from the curse of the law. But is this functionally true? Or is there still some legal claim that the devil is making against us? It is important that we thoroughly investigate the Word of God. We mustn't just look for scriptures to back up our own particular theological position. We must be people who look for truth and desire it intensely.

As I travel the world and speak on *The Courts of Heaven*, many times I encounter people who want to argue. Their main contention with my teaching is that Jesus *legally* did everything that was necessary for our complete and total salvation on the cross. I honestly have no problem with this. I recognize the immense work of Jesus on my behalf. This is the cause of my salvation and deliverance. However, satan is a legalist. The apostle Peter, who walked with Jesus, tells us that satan is still seeking a *legal right* to devour us. First Peter 5:8 is explicit concerning this:

> *Be sober, be vigilant; because your adversary the devil walks about like a roaring lion, seeking whom he may devour.*

The word *adversary* is the Greek word *antidikos*. This word literally means "an opponent in a lawsuit." The devil is bringing a *lawsuit* against us. Peter is declaring this *after* the cross. To be clear, the devil *still* claims a right and power to operate as one who *legally* can devour us! Peter is urging us to be on guard and vigilant in protecting ourselves against this. Satan's power to devour is a result of legal claims against us. However, we have the right to take all that Jesus did for us and silence those claims. This is our privilege and right as those who are born again and have been purchased by the blood of the Lamb!

Another factor in understanding curses is to realize that the full redemption from curses has not yet come. Again, we realize based on Galatians 3:13 that Jesus's atoning work *legally* delivered us from the curses listed in the law. Yet it is not until the millennial reign of Jesus comes that *all* curses are revoked and removed. Revelation 22:1-3 gives us this insight.

> *And he showed me a pure river of water of life, clear as crystal, proceeding from the throne of God and of the Lamb. In the middle of its street, and on either side of the river, was the tree of life, which bore twelve fruits, each tree yielding its fruit every month. The leaves of the tree were for the healing of the nations. And there shall be no more curse,*

*but the throne of God and of the Lamb shall
be in it, and His servants shall serve Him.*

The pure river of Life flows from the throne of God. We should know that the flow of the Holy Spirit is always connected to the rulership of the Lord. Wherever the throne of God is established, there will be a free flow of God's presence from that place. If God's throne is established in us, then from us will proceed the river of Life that brings great life to others.

This has always been the challenge of the Lord to me. I must allow His throne as Lord of all to be established in my life. When I do, the life-giving flow of God will manifest in me and through me. Notice that when the rule of God is absolutely established, not only will there be great fruitfulness, but there will also be *no more curse*. We will not see *no more curses* operating in the earth or people's lives *until* the millennial reign of Jesus begins. Then God's throne will be fully set in place and every right of curses to operate will be annulled. The full enforcement of all that Jesus legally did on the cross will be recognized at this time. The legal work of Jesus will be fully executed into place. The right of curses to operate on any level will then be revoked! The new Heaven and new earth will be set in place.

So what does this mean? It means that Jesus's work on the cross was complete and absolutely sufficient. However, the full execution of it will not be seen until He comes again. His work on the cross was everything that was legally necessary for a full redemption. However, the fullness of that redemption is not yet seen. Until that day of complete redemption and reclaiming of all things back to God, there will be curses. It is up to us to take what Jesus did and annul those curses and deny them their right to operate! We have everything we need through the blood and body of Jesus to revoke curses against us. We can free ourselves, our families, and even culture from the effects of curses. Jesus's body and blood given in His atoning work are that powerful. Curses will not dictate our future.

Our families will not be ruled because of some legal claim of the devil against us. We will see the deliverance of the Lord and His freedom become ours.

Chapter 1

CURSES AND THE COURTS OF HEAVEN

In the introduction, we discussed and sought to establish that curses operate from a legal basis. We must take the legal work of Jesus and implement and execute it. Then, all that Jesus died for us to have can be ours in a practical sense. In the next chapter, we will see the imperative work of the Holy Spirit to accomplish this. First, however, I want to give us a basis for operating in the Courts of Heaven. The Courts of Heaven are not an imaginary place. I believe it to be as real a place as any natural court could be. In Daniel 7:9-10, we see Daniel as a seer "seeing" into the unseen realm and witnessing the Courts of Heaven.

I watched till thrones were put in place, and the Ancient of Days was seated; His garment was white as snow, and the hair of His head was like pure wool. His throne was a fiery flame, its wheels a burning fire; a fiery stream issued and came forth from before Him. A thousand thousands ministered to Him; ten thousand times ten thousand stood before Him. The court was seated, and the books were opened.

These verses show Daniel *watching* as the Courts of Heaven come to operation. He sees thrones, fiery flames, burning fiery wheels, fiery streams, books being opened, and myriads of beings ministering to the Ancient of Days who is seated on His throne. I understand this to all be literal and in existence in the spirit world. Everything about the Courts of Heaven has meaning. For instance, three different references are made to *fire* in some form or fashion. His throne is a fiery flame. Wheels in the throne are a burning fire. Fiery streams are issued and come forth before Him. I believe these fiery streams are verdicts and justice being rendered from His throne. Psalm 97:2-3 tells us that fiery judgments go out from the Lord.

Clouds and darkness surround Him; righteousness and justice are the foundation of His throne. A fire goes before Him, and burns up His enemies round about.

Notice that the fire that is burning up the enemies is connected to the righteousness and justice of the throne.

I had never had this thought before. I was in a meeting in which I was asked to take the prophecy that was being released and present it as a case in the Courts of Heaven. As the prophets spoke, I recorded their words to present before the Courts of Heaven. I understood that these prophetic words were coming from the open books that we also see in Daniel. It was the prophets' job to perceive from the open books. It was my job, apostolically, to take those words and present them to the Courts for righteous judgments.

As I began to petition the Courts of Heaven based on the prophetic revelation, this deep groaning and roar began to come out of me. I had experienced this some before, but I had never experienced it on this level. As I began to petition the Courts of Heaven and groan under the weight of His power, I heard the Spirit declare, "*A fiery stream issues and goes forth before Him.*" I knew at that moment that the Courts of Heaven were issuing a judgment on behalf of the prophetic revelation with which I was petitioning the Courts. It was a fiery stream that would go forth before Him and burn up His enemies. Whatever was against God and His purposes was in jeopardy of being consumed by the judgments flowing from His throne. This happened because people who belonged to Jesus were petitioning the Courts of Heaven.

We have a right to approach the Courts of Heaven and make our case before Him. We can see the works of the devil that have been set against us consumed and burned up. This includes curses that are sent to consume our lives, futures, and destinies. He will send forth His fiery stream to consume His enemies.

We must recognize that we as New Testament believers have been given the right to approach this Court we see in the book of Daniel. This is why Jesus placed prayer in a judicial setting in Luke 18:1-8. He was directly and indirectly communicating that prayer can be legal activity before the Courts of Heaven. Jesus hid many wonderful truths in this parable.

> Then He spoke a parable to them, that men always ought to pray and not lose heart, saying: "There was in a certain city a judge who did not fear God nor regard man. Now there was a widow in that city; and she came to him, saying, 'Get justice for me from my adversary.' And he would not for a while; but afterward he said within himself, 'Though I do not fear God nor regard man, yet because this widow troubles me I will avenge her, lest by her continual coming she weary me.'"

Then the Lord said, "Hear what the unjust judge said. And shall God not avenge His own elect who cry out day and night to Him, though He bears long with them? I tell you that He will avenge them speedily. Nevertheless, when the Son of Man comes, will He really find faith on the earth?"

The first thing we must recognize is that the Courts of Heaven are not a method of praying but a spiritual dimension. I cover this at length in my book *Father, Friend, and Judge.* I talk about knowing how to come by faith before God in these three areas. Each one is a different spiritual dimension. When we approach God as Father, we come into the *secret place.* When we approach God as Friend, we step into the *counsel of the Lord.* When we approach God as Judge, we come into the *Courts of Heaven.* This is the spiritual dimension that Daniel saw and reported. We are given the right to petition God as Judge by standing in this spiritual realm—the Courts of Heaven.

The second thing we should know is that we have access to this holy place because of Jesus's blood shed for us. Hebrews 10:19 clearly tells us that we get to enter into the holiest place by and through the sacrificial blood of Jesus. I don't have to be good enough. I can come before Him because of the blood that has made me a new creation and righteous.

Therefore, brethren, having boldness to enter the Holiest by the blood of Jesus.

We can boldly approach God in all of His holiness because of what the blood has legally done for us. Which brings me to my third thing that we must know. The Courts of Heaven are *for the elect.* When Jesus spoke the parable about the widow and the unjust judge, He said, "How much more will God avenge His own *elect.*" In other words, the whole story He told was to encourage the *elect* or *chosen* that the Courts of Heaven are a place for them. It is a place in the spirit world where we can petition God and see judgments come against the powers of darkness. Any and every legal claim that has been made to land curses can be revoked and removed. God will avenge them speedily. This means He will render judgments against the powers of darkness and cause them to lose any right they are claiming. This is all done from a real place in the spirit world called the Courts of Heaven. We have been given access into it and shall not be denied operation there. It is our blood-purchased, legal right. Let's enter with boldness and see every legal claim of curses revoked.

As I come before Your Courts, Lord, I thank You that I have entrance because of the blood of Jesus. Your precious blood gives me the right to stand in this place before You. I come as the elect and chosen of God. I ask that my enemy and legal opponent might be judged as illegal and unrighteous. That he would be deemed legally unfit to bring a case or assault against me. Let my right to stand in this holy place be established before You. I am Your vessel, and therefore Your blood does speak for me. Let it be recorded that by faith I believe I can stand in this spiritual dimension because of all that You, Lord, have done for me. Therefore, let every curse lose its right to operate against me and my generations from this place. In Jesus's name, amen!

Chapter 2

HOLY SPIRIT: MY LEGAL AID

When Jesus died on the cross, He legally accomplished everything necessary for our complete salvation. This is what we are told in 2 Peter 1:3.

As His divine power has given to us all things that pertain to life and godliness, through the knowledge of Him who called us by glory and virtue.

Notice the tense of this statement. Everything that pertains to life and godliness has *already* been given to us. This means that Jesus legally purchased everything for us through His death on the cross. However, we do not see these provisions become ours without the person and power of the Holy Spirit. What has legally been procured must be executed into place. We see this in what Jesus said in John 16:8-11.

> And when He has come, He will convict the world of sin, and of righteousness, and of judgment: of sin, because they do not believe in Me; of righteousness, because I go to My Father and you see Me no more; of judgment, because the ruler of this world is judged.

Speaking of the Holy Spirit, Jesus showed three things He would do when He came. The word *convict* in the Greek is *elegcho*. It can mean "to convince." The Holy Spirit will *convince* us of three very significant things. He will first *convince* us concerning the sin of unbelief. The Holy Spirit will declare war against our unbelief. He will seek to move us into real faith that is required to access the provisions of the covenant we have in God through the blood of Jesus. He will deliver us from an evil heart of unbelief. Hebrews 3:12 speaks of this evil heart.

Beware, brethren, lest there be in any of you an evil heart of unbelief in departing from the living God.

We tend to dismiss the seriousness of our unbelief. Yet the Bible tells us that unbelief flows from an evil heart. Jesus actually challenged the disciples because of their unbelief in His post-resurrection form. Mark 16:14 reveals Jesus strongly rebuking them for not believing.

Later He appeared to the eleven as they sat at the table; and He rebuked their unbelief and hardness of heart, because they did not believe those who had seen Him after He had risen.

Somehow we think it is spiritual to question things and demand proof. However, Jesus loves it when we choose to believe. Notice that unbelief is connected to hardness of heart. I never want to be a cynic and skeptic. I what to have a soft, pliable heart that believes God. The Holy Spirit will create this in me as I give Him room and space to occupy my heart.

The second thing Jesus revealed the Holy Spirit would do is convince us of righteousness. When Jesus was with the disciples, they had a living depiction of righteousness. Jesus showed through His life what caused people to be in right standing with the Lord. Jesus said that in His absence the Holy Spirit would be the One to show them what real righteousness is. This is important. Left to our own devices, we will either become lawless or legalists. The Bible speaks of the path of righteousness in Psalm 23:3.

He restores my soul; He leads me in the paths of righteousness for His name's sake.

Every path has ditches on either side. Without the Holy Spirit's influence, we will end up in the ditch of lawlessness or the ditch of legalism. It is the job of the Holy Spirit to help define the true path of righteousness that we are to walk in. He causes us to know how to apply the Word of God in our life.

The third aspect of the Holy Spirit's ministry that Jesus spoke of was convincing us that the ruler of this world is judged! When Jesus died on the cross, judgment came against satan as the ruler of this world. Every work of his was deemed illegal, unrighteous, and immoral. He killed the Son of God, who was sinless and without fault. Up until that time, everyone else who was killed, harmed, and wounded through satan's activities could be said to deserve it. We are all guilty and deserving of death. However, when satan killed Jesus on the cross, he killed an innocent and righteous man who is God. Satan could now be judged as the murderer, liar, and thief that he is. Jesus gave His life for us. When He died on the cross, God could now righteously judge satan and all his works. The cross was in essence a verdict against the powers of darkness. This is what several scriptures declare. For instance, Hebrews 2:14 declares that through His death Jesus destroyed satan's right to bring death.

Inasmuch then as the children have partaken of flesh and blood, He Himself likewise shared in the same, that through death He might destroy him who had the power of death, that is, the devil.

Even though satan has been legally destroyed, he is still operating today. This is because the legal verdict of the cross has not been fully executed into place. This will not completely occur until satan is cast into the lake of fire and brimstone. Revelation 20:10 gives us this declaration.

The devil, who deceived them, was cast into the lake of fire and brimstone where the beast and the false prophet are. And they will be tormented day and night forever and ever.

This is the fullness of the verdict of the cross against satan. Up until this time, we must actively set into place the verdict of the cross. This allows us to have in fullness the benefit of that which is yet to come. This is actually what we do in the Courts of Heaven. We state our case and remind the Courts of the *finished work* of Jesus. This allows us to get the full effect of the legal verdict rendered from the cross.

The judgment of the cross against satan is sure. His legal right to bring death is revoked. First John 3:8 also tells us that Jesus's manifestation destroyed the works of the devil.

He who sins is of the devil, for the devil has sinned from the beginning. For this purpose the Son of God was manifested, that He might destroy the works of the devil.

The word *destroy* in the Greek is *luo*. It has legal connotations. It means:

- laws, as having a binding force, are likened to bonds
- to annul, subvert

- to do away with, to deprive of authority, whether by precept or act

- to declare unlawful

Clearly Jesus was manifested and revealed to legally annul and revoke the works and activities of satan. The challenge is to get the legal verdict of Jesus's work into place. This is why Jesus declared that the Holy Spirit has come to convince us of the judgment and verdict of the cross. The Holy Spirit is our legal aid to execute into place all that Jesus legally did on the cross. This is very important. If we are to see curses broken off our lives and families, it requires the Holy Spirit's activity in our life.

Jesus declared in John 14:16 that the Spirit is our *Helper*.

And I will pray the Father, and He will give you another Helper, that He may abide with you forever.

Helper in this scripture is the Greek word *parakletos*. It means "an intercessor and a consoler." It also means "a legal aid." This is the same word that is used for Jesus being our advocate in 1 John 2:1.

> My little children, these things I write to you, so that you may not sin. And if anyone sins, we have an Advocate with the Father, Jesus Christ the righteous.

This is a reference to Jesus functioning as our lawyer/attorney before the Courts of Heaven. However, the Holy Spirit is here with us to empower us to set in place all that Jesus has legally done. Jesus is operating in the heavenly place, while the Holy Spirit as our legal aid is helping us get things in place in the earthly realm. We see the judgments of Jesus from the cross set in place against the powers of darkness. The Holy Spirit is the one who helps us execute these judgments into reality.

I can give you three secrets to equip you to move in agreement with the Holy Spirit. First of all, we must not be ignorant of His ways. First Corinthians 12:1 shows Paul instructing people about how the Spirit operates. One of the critical issues in today's church is that we don't understand how to agree with the Spirit. Therefore, we inadvertently quench and grieve Him.

> *Now concerning spiritual gifts, brethren, I do not want you to be ignorant.*

Two things can make us ignorant of how the Spirit moves and prohibit us from moving with Him. One is the way we were raised in our youth. The other is our religious training. If we were forced in our youth to quell our emotions, this can hinder our cooperation with the Spirit of the Lord. If we were caused to feel that emotions were made to be held in check rather than expressed in a healthy manner, this will stop us from agreeing with the Holy Spirit. If emotions were considered to be a sign of weakness, this would stigmatize them in our own minds. Therefore, we would have learned to shut down our emotions. This is a problem when seeking to cooperate with the Spirit of

God. Our emotions are not the Spirit of the Lord, but our emotions are energized by the Spirit's movement. If I squelch the emotions and don't give room to them, I can also squelch and quench the move of the Holy Spirit.

In regard to religious training, if we were taught that piety was to be a quiet and personal matter, this can hinder the move of the Spirit. The denominational church I grew up in didn't make room for the move of the Holy Spirit. In fact, it was very legalistic in its beliefs and what it espoused. Therefore, my belief system concerning how the Spirit of God moves was fashioned by those early influences. I had to break free from the idea that God only did things quietly or that anything that had volume or an emotional display was not the Spirit of the Lord.

A man once said about the move of the Holy Spirit, "God is not deaf." Another person responded, "Yes, but neither is He nervous." The first person's point was that loudness and emotionalism don't necessarily mean something is from God. However, as the second person pointed out, neither does it negate or declare something is not God.

Through the course of my life, I have learned to enjoy the emotions the Holy Spirit inspires. I have also learned that the move of God's Holy Spirit can be soft and gentle yet powerful. I have again learned that the Holy Spirit can also cause loud and unorthodox responses out of people. If we can learn this concerning the Spirit of the Lord, we can be free from ignorance of how the Spirit moves. We can be instructed in how to yield to the Spirit of God and experience the touch of His presence. This will deliver us from curses and accomplish the work of God in our heart. The Spirit will be free to execute the full verdict of the cross against the powers of darkness.

A second secret to the Holy Spirit operating as our legal aid and setting in place all Jesus did for us is communing with Him. Second Corinthians 13:14 shows us that the Holy Spirit desires to fellowship with us.

The grace of the Lord Jesus Christ, and the love of God, and the communion of the Holy Spirit be with you all. Amen.

The word *communion* is the Greek word *koinonia*. It means "partnership, participation, and distribution." When we talk of fellowship and communion with the Spirit of God, we aren't just speaking about *feeling* His presence. We are speaking of working together with Him in partnership. We are a participant in whatever He is seeking to accomplish. In other words, our faith, activity, and involvement are necessary to execute the finished work of Jesus! Through the Holy Spirit and my fellowship with Him, I discern what He is doing and come into agreement with that. When I do this, I get the benefit of all Jesus legally accomplished on the cross. This is basically the way Jesus operated as He walked the earth. In John 5:19, Jesus declared His absolute dependence on discerning what the Father was doing from the heavenly realm. When He discerned it and agreed with it, miraculous things happened.

Then Jesus answered and said to them, "Most assuredly, I say to you, the Son can do nothing of Himself, but what He sees the Father do; for whatever He does, the Son also does in like manner."

This was in response to healing the man at the pool of Bethesda. Jesus declared the simplicity of it. He simply recognized what His Father was doing and came into agreement with it. This is what we do as we commune, participate in, and distribute the work of God through the Holy Spirit. The Spirit is then free to use us to execute the work of the cross into absolute reality.

The third secret to the Holy Spirit executing the finished work of Jesus is to realize our complete dependence on Him. There was a reason why Jesus told His disciples to wait for empowerment. It was because they would need the Holy Spirit's power to do the work and complete their God-ordained task. Luke 24:49 shows Jesus instructing these disciples to tarry for the power.

Behold, I send the Promise of My Father upon you; but tarry in the city of Jerusalem until you are endued with power from on high.

This was, of course, Jesus preparing them for the coming of the Holy Spirit on the Day of Pentecost. He was communicating to them that the Holy Spirit's coming was going to change everything. They would go from fearful to fearless. They would go from powerless to powerful. They would go from awful to amazing. All this would happen because of the empowerment of the Spirit of God that would come upon them.

This scripture gives us some insight into what actually happened when the Holy Spirit came in as the sound of a rushing mighty wind. The word *tarry* in the Greek is the word *kathizo*. It means "to sit down." It is the idea of a king *sitting down on a throne*. When the Holy Spirit came, He was going to bring not just power but also a place of authority in the spiritual world. From this position in the spiritual realm, they would alter life on the planet. The anointing that would flow from the disciples would come from the recognized position they occupied in the heavenly dimension. They would take a seat of authority.

This scripture also says they would be *endued* with power. This word *endued* in the Greek is *enduo* and it means "to invest with clothing, to sink into a garment." Not only would they be seated in the spirit world, but the Spirit of God would clothe them like a garment. He would be a mantle that empowered their lives. This would allow them to execute the finished work of Jesus through the power of the Spirit! The empowerment of the Holy Spirit allows us the precious honor and privilege of setting into proper place all that Jesus has legally done. When we do this, curses are broken and the power of satan is annulled. People go free because of all that Jesus has legally done and the anointing of the Holy Spirit to bring it into reality.

As I stand in Your Courts today, I call into remembrance all the work of Jesus on the cross. May it be recorded that I believe in the finished work of Jesus from the cross. I believe that everything that legally needed to be done, Jesus has done for me. I ask also that it might be recorded that I know the Holy Spirit is my legal aid. He is the One who functionally sets into place all that Jesus legally has accomplished for me. I ask that I might agree and cooperate with the Holy Spirit so that every precious thing Jesus did will operate for me. Let every curse be annulled, revoked, and lose the right to function against me and my family. Let the power of the Holy Spirit set in place the full work of Jesus for me. In Jesus's name, amen!

Chapter 3

THE CAUSE OF INIQUITY

A re curses the source of my frustration and even inability to live a peaceful life? Are curses stopping me from fulfilling the destiny ordained by God for me? What are the signs of a curse? What is a good definition of a curse? These are all questions that should be asked and answered.

First of all, a good definition for *curse* is "a negative spiritual force sabotaging God's plan for my life by taking advantage of legal rights claimed by the demonic." In other words, a curse is real and it is out to destroy every good thing God intended for us. However, it can only work from a legal place in the spirit world. Proverbs 26:2 declares that curses operating against a person or people must have a *cause.*

Like a flitting sparrow, like a flying swallow,
so a curse without cause shall not alight.

The *cause* of a curse is that the demonic has discovered a legal claim to bring it into place. Notice that curses are likened to birds looking for a place to land. It is up to us not to allow a landing place for these curses. There can be a myriad of causes the devil might discover to land curses against us. However, I want to look at three distinct reasons that are the most common—iniquity, covenants, and words. I have discovered that these three are expressly used to destroy the intent of God in people and families. Any of these three can be something we are guilty of in our present time or something someone in our generations was guilty of.

Remember that the devil is not omniscient or all-knowing. However, he can commission an investigation to search our lives and/or history. This is very much like an attorney or law firm hiring investigators to find evidence against someone. They can search the history of someone to locate damning information. Satan does this as well to find anything legal that can be used against us. He authorizes the demonic powers at his fingertips to search and locate certain things that would grant him a legal right. This is especially true when someone becomes a threat to him and his agenda. He has to find a legal claim against them that can be used to stop them.

This is what happened to me. I had led a very successful local work that we had birthed and raised up. It was a powerful expression of God's kingdom power. After 15 years of leading this work, the Lord clearly instructed us to step away from it and for me to begin to travel. This was going to launch me into a kingdom level ministry to the world. God wanted to increase my sphere to touch the nations. I was excited about this but had no idea of the attack I was going to come under.

We had fought many battles in the 15 years of leading a local expression of the church. We had come to a place of great blessing, prosperity, and breakthrough. The house we had helped build was filled with the glory and presence of the Lord. In fact, the Lord showed me that the anointing in the house was like the house of Obed-Edom. This was where David put the ark when he tried to bring it up in a wrong manner. It stayed there for three months. The house of Obed-Edom was greatly blessed. Second Samuel 6:11-12 says everything in the house of Obed-Edom was blessed. His whole household was under the blessing of the Lord because of the awesome presence of God that was there.

The ark of the Lord remained in the house of Obed-Edom the Gittite three months. And the Lord blessed Obed-Edom and all his household.

Now it was told King David, saying, "The Lord has blessed the house of Obed-Edom and all that belongs to him, because of the ark of God." So David went and brought up the ark of God from the house of Obed-Edom to the City of David with gladness.

When David heard how great the blessing was on that house, he went and moved the ark. He repositioned the ark on the Hill of Zion. In that place, the ark that had blessed a house began to bless a nation. The presence or anointing didn't get bigger; it was just repositioned for a greater effect and influence.

This is what the Lord did with me. It wasn't that the anointing on my life increased; it was that I was repositioned from a *house* to a *hill*. In a house, I had the privilege of touching a city and region. From a hill, I was given the honor of impacting nations. It wasn't about new levels of anointing. It was about a new positioning to use the anointing I already carried to affect new dimensions for the Lord.

You may not need a new anointing. Maybe you need a new positioning. What the Lord has birthed in you can have the potential to touch nations. The devil knew this. As I was repositioned to take what I carried in God to now touch nations, he intended to stop this. His method against me was to search out my ancestry and find legal claims to land curses. The result of this was that our life began to fall apart. My reputation came under attack. My children began to make unwise and fleshly decisions. Our marriage began to falter. Finances dried up. About anything you can imagine other than sickness and death started to hit us.

The problem was that I couldn't get it stopped. For 30-plus years, I had been a disciplined man of prayer. I had a place in God that could stop attacks and get breakthroughs. In this time, however, nothing worked. No matter how much I prayed or what strategies I employed, everything kept getting worse. Before I could get one problem solved, five more had piled on top of that one. I later learned this was a true sign of a curse at work. The devil had discovered a legal right to resist any kingdom impact I was destined for. I was to discover that much of what was allowing these attacks were legal claims from my ancestry.

So what are the three primary areas the devil uses as a legal claim to land curses? What is the legal cause he discovers? The first right that he claims is *iniquity in the bloodline.* Iniquity is the sin of our ancestors. Iniquity is one of the primary legal reasons the devil can bring curses against us. The Bible is clear that the iniquity of our fathers can be used to affect us today. In fact, whatever we are today is a result of our ancestry. We are a byproduct of those who have gone before us, both good and bad. Those who lived righteous and noble lives allow us to claim their effect. For instance, Timothy had a faith "inherited" from his family line. Paul spoke of this in 2 Timothy 1:5.

When I call to remembrance the genuine faith that is in you, which dwelt first in your grandmother Lois and your mother Eunice, and I am persuaded is in you also.

Timothy had claims to a dynamic faith because of the faith-filled way his grandmother and mother had lived. We need to know how to go into the Courts of Heaven and claim these kinds of things for ourselves. I believe much good from our family lines is unclaimed. We miss out on what could be ours. We can go before His Courts and ask for the blessing and empowerment that flow from this realm. However, just like there are good things that flow from our family history, there are also bad. The devil knows how to make cases against us based on our family sins and iniquities. This can be found in several scriptures. Exodus 20:4-5 gives us this insight concerning the right of the devil to visit the effects of sin against us from our ancestry.

You shall not make for yourself a carved image—any likeness of anything that is in heaven above, or that is in the earth beneath, or that is in the water under the earth; you shall not bow down to them nor serve them. For I, the Lord your God, am a jealous God, visiting the iniquity of the fathers upon the children to the third and fourth generations of those who hate Me.

These statements from the Lord grant the devil the legal right to land curses against us based on the iniquity in our bloodline. The devil can only use the Word of God to bring cases against us. He must find a violation of God's law in us or our bloodline. This is why Jesus said the devil had searched Him out and found nothing in John 14:30.

I will no longer talk much with you, for the ruler of this world is coming, and he has nothing in Me.

This statement of Jesus implies that there was no sin in Him or His bloodline that satan could use against Him. This was because Jesus lived a perfect and sinless life. Plus, Jesus's lineage was from God. He was conceived by the Holy Spirit. He had no natural father whose bloodline could be used against Him. Therefore, satan had no legal recourse against Jesus. Satan had searched Him out and found nothing. However, this is not true of us. We all have sinned and fallen short of the glory of God. Plus, we have compromised bloodlines that allow accusations against us. We also see this in Leviticus 26:39.

> *And those of you who are left shall waste away in their iniquity in your enemies' lands; also in their fathers' iniquities, which are with them, they shall waste away.*

Notice that the fathers' iniquities will cause us to waste away. The devil claims a legal right against us to land curses that progressively destroy our lives and destinies. Ezekiel 18:30 makes a powerful statement about the effect of iniquity in our bloodline.

"Therefore I will judge you, O house of Israel, every one according to his ways," says the Lord God. "Repent, and turn from all your transgressions, so that iniquity will not be your ruin."

Iniquity in our bloodline will allow the devil to bring ruin to our lives. This is the legal claim the devil uses against us to ruin our lives. This is why so many lives filled with hope and promise come to ruin. According to John 10:10, the devil as the thief comes to steal, kill, and destroy.

The thief does not come except to steal, and to kill, and to destroy. I have come that they may have life, and that they may have it more abundantly.

Just like the devil desires and intends to annihilate any good in our life, Jesus has come to stop that and bring us life! He will cause the intentions of the devil to be stopped. He will instead bring us life and that with much abundance.

I know someone whose life illustrates iniquity in the bloodline. This particular lady was a pastor and had watched several of her siblings die premature deaths. They had all come tragically to death before their time. Finally, the grandmother of the family came to this lady and told her a story she knew nothing about. It seemed that decades before, her grandfather had gotten into a bar fight and killed a man with a knife. The grandmother had then watched person after person be removed from their family through sickness, violence, and other means of death. The grandmother had an intuitive sense that it was related to the violent act of the grandfather who had killed that man. The pastor immediately knew what the Word of God says. The law of God is explicit in Genesis 9:6. If someone kills a person, then they must be killed or die prematurely.

Whoever sheds man's blood, by man his blood shall be shed; for in the image of God He made man.

When these kinds of statements are made in the Word of God, the devil will take them and use them to build a case against us. He will claim this over a person and their coming generations. This lady pastor knew she must go into the Courts of Heaven and undo the legal claim the devil was making. She did this and immediately all premature death stopped. The curse of premature and untimely deaths caused by sickness and disease and violence came to an end in that family. People became free to live out their lives to the fullness of days.

Any place where there has been a violation of God's Word and law the devil will use this against us. When the accusers in Jesus's day brought the woman caught in adultery, they were using Moses law against her. In John 8:4-5, they claimed a legal right to kill her.

They said to Him, "Teacher, this woman was caught in adultery, in the very act. Now Moses, in the law, commanded us that such should be stoned. But what do You say?"

They were seeking to find a way to accuse Jesus. In this scripture, we see how those who were of the spirit of satan used the Word of God against this woman. Their case against her was based on her violation of God's word. This is exactly what the devil does to us. Any legal claim against us is based on our violation of God's word or the violations in our ancestry. We must repent for any and all places where satan can make claims against us. When this is done, the legal right to land curses is removed.

In the next chapters, we will deal with the other two prevalent reasons for curses—demonic covenants and word curses. For now, here is a prayer that can help revoke legal claims to land curses based upon iniquity in our bloodline.

Lord, as I come before Your Courts of Heaven, I acknowledge my sin and the iniquity of my bloodline. I acknowledge that we were all sinners. Yet, Lord, Your precious blood has cleansed me of my sin and speaks on behalf of my bloodline. I ask that any and every voice against me in the spirit world or the natural would now be silenced before You. Let it be known that I am Yours by the purchasing of Your blood.

I repent for my sins and the sins of my bloodline. Any curse against me that is taking opportunity through the sins of my ancestry, let its rights be revoked. Let every landing place of any curse now be removed, because the cause or legal right has been annulled. I ask that anything that has been stolen from me by the thief, satan, would now be returned. I remind these Courts that the thief came to steal, kill, and destroy. However, You, Lord, came to give abundant life. Let all that I have lost by and through the legal claims of the devil now be restored plus more in Jesus's name, amen.

Chapter 4

DEMONIC COVENANTS

Throughout the years of researching, praying, and operating in the Courts of Heaven, I have come to a conclusion: One of the greatest causes of curses is covenants with the devil made in our ancestral history. The problem with this is that most of us would never believe such a thing about ourselves or our family. We are appalled at the idea that someone would have done something so overtly evil as this. However, these covenants can be made intentionally or unintentionally. If they are in place, it gives the devil the legal right to claim us and our lineage after us.

One of the important things about iniquity is that it has a statute of limitations attached to it. God Himself said that iniquity, or sin in the bloodline, can only be used against us for four generations. Again, Exodus 20:4-5 expresses this.

> *You shall not make for yourself a carved image—any likeness of anything that is in heaven above, or that is in the earth beneath, or that is in the water under the earth; you shall not bow down to them nor serve them. For I, the Lord your God, am a jealous God, visiting the iniquity of the fathers upon the children to the third and fourth generations of those who hate Me.*

This is why we have the right to come before the Courts of Heaven and request that God's statute of limitations be set into place. We petition the Courts and ask that nothing past four generations can be used against us to land a curse. This is important. If the devil has access to and can land curses from iniquity all the way back to Adam and Eve, then it is a never-ending task to deal with these issues. However, if only iniquity for four generations is admissible in the Courts of Heaven, we can deal with this. We can go before the Courts of Heaven and repent and ask that these sins in our ancestry be revoked from being used against us. The devil therefore loses the legal claim to land curses against on the basis of iniquity. The only exclusion to this is found in Deuteronomy 23:2. This scripture says that one born illegitimately or outside marriage cannot enter the congregation. They are expelled and rejected.

> *One of illegitimate birth shall not enter the assembly of the Lord; even to the tenth generation none of his descendants shall enter the assembly of the Lord.*

This is one of the reasons people suffer from a rejection complex. Somewhere in their bloodline there was illegitimate birth. The devil claims this as a legal right to afflict them with rejection and purposelessness. This should be taken into the Courts to have these claims revoked and removed. This is the one exception to iniquity being visited for four generations. This one issue can be upon a family line for ten generations. The devil is a legalist and will use this word against us. He will seek to visit iniquity. Yet there are statutes of limitations we should call into effect to restrict his intent!

Covenants with demons are different. They are perpetual in nature until they are undone. This is because of what God has said about covenants. Covenants are forever and are passed from generation to generation. Psalm 105:7-8 tells us from a legal perspective that a covenant is an everlasting thing.

He is the Lord our God; His judgments are in all the earth. He remembers His covenant forever, the word which He commanded, for a thousand generations.

The word *judgments* in the Hebrew is *mishpat.* It means "a judicial verdict." Our God is a legal God. Therefore, He remembers and is faithful to His covenant forever. When the

Lord says He keeps covenant for a thousand generations, it is simply another way of saying it lasts forever. This is an awesome and reassuring truth. He will be faithful to us always. However, when God sets this standard for covenant, the devil uses it to claim the same right. He declares that if God says covenants last forever, then any covenant made with him can be exacted forever as well. This is why a covenant with the demonic is a perpetual thing. Whereas iniquity has time limitations on it, a covenant in the bloodline does not. Any covenant made with demons knowingly or unknowingly lasts until we stop it. This is the source of many curses, and it has given the devil a legal right to curse our lives.

We have examples in Scripture of God's people making covenants with demons. Isaiah 28:14-15 shows scornful leaders seeking demonic help through covenants and agreements.

Therefore hear the word of the Lord, you scornful men, who rule this people who are in

Jerusalem, because you have said, "We have made a covenant with death, and with Sheol we are in agreement. When the overflowing scourge passes through, it will not come to us, for we have made lies our refuge, and under falsehood we have hidden ourselves."

Notice that the purpose of this covenant was for protection and safety. They were sure that the demon powers would protect and guard them. Trouble and enemies would not be able to touch them because of their agreement with devils. These same things are happening today. Leaders of nations have secretly come into covenant with demon powers. They are empowered by these devils to accomplish their agenda and stay in control. However, this releases curses upon the people who are under their leadership. Whole nations suffer because of the covenants leaders have with demon powers to hold on to authority. We as the church must know how to go before the Courts of Heaven and deal with these atrocities.

However, individual families are also under curses because of covenants in their bloodline made with demons. We can also see a reference to these covenants in 1 Kings 19:18 where God is correcting Elijah. Elijah thinks he's the only one who is not serving the demon god Baal. Yet God lets him know this isn't true. He has 7,000 prophets and servants who are instead serving the Lord.

Yet I have reserved seven thousand in Israel, all whose knees have not bowed to Baal, and every mouth that has not kissed him.

God says there are these 7,000 who have not surrendered and offered offerings to Baal or worshiped him. These activities would have made a covenant with this demonic hierarchy. There was a whole culture of Israel that had sold out to serve Baal. Their covenant with him empowered his rulership and influence over Israel. This happens on a family level as well.

Covenants are made through sacrifice. This is the standard in God's Word in Psalm 50:5.

Gather My saints together to Me, those who have made a covenant with Me by sacrifice.

Just like covenants are made with the Lord through sacrifice, so it is with the demonic. Of course, Jesus made a covenant with us by His magnificent sacrifice on the cross. His body and blood caused us to come into a covenant with Him and the Godhead. We have a covenant relationship because of the great sacrifice of Jesus on our behalf. However, people make covenants with demons wittingly and unwittingly as well. For instance, if we or someone in our bloodline is guilty of innocent bloodshed, the demons take this as a legal right to claim a covenant with us. Abortion and any other shedding of blood in our bloodline can allow the dark powers to insist they have a legal right to us. This is because the shedding of blood makes covenant. It is no accident that the covenant we have with God required the shedding of Jesus's innocent blood. Hebrews 10:29 refers to the power of this blood. It shows us that it must be treated and respected as holy.

> *Of how much worse punishment, do you suppose, will he be thought worthy who has trampled the Son of God underfoot, counted the blood of the covenant by which he was sanctified a common thing, and insulted the Spirit of grace?*

Whoever treats the *blood of the covenant* as an unholy thing is in danger of eternal punishment. This is because of the sacredness of His precious blood. However, all blood is valuable. It is the costliest and most valuable commodity in the universe. When innocent blood is shed, demons can claim a legal right on that basis. This is most definitely true when it is done with intent and on purpose. However, even when it is done without the awareness of the spiritual reality connected to it, the demonic will still claim covenantal rights against us. We must know how to go before the Courts of Heaven and revoke the legal claim against us based on bloodshed in our bloodline.

Money can also be a sacrifice that makes covenant with demons. For instance, I have had to break covenants I had with demons because of money that was sown into religious organizations. Some would say, "What? Aren't they from God?" The fact is that demons infiltrate and influence religious organizations and churches. Jesus warned of this when He spoke about the mustard seed that became a huge tree in Matthew 13:31-32.

Another parable He put forth to them, saying: "The kingdom of heaven is like a mustard seed, which a man took and sowed in his field, which indeed is the least of all the seeds; but when it is grown it is greater than the herbs and becomes a tree, so that the birds of the air come and nest in its branches."

Notice that this seed, which started small, increased and grew until it became a tree. The tree then became a house for birds to lodge in.

We know that in parables birds are symbolic of demons. Matthew 13:4 tells us that the birds come and devour the seed of the kingdom.

And as he sowed, some seed fell by the wayside; and the birds came and devoured them.

Jesus interprets this parable for the disciples in Matthew 13:19.

When anyone hears the word of the kingdom, and does not understand it, then the wicked one comes and snatches away what was sown in his heart. This is he who received seed by the wayside.

Jesus clearly says that the birds that steal away the seed sown by the wayside are the *wicked one.* This is a reference to demonic powers. The parable of the sower has symbols that are consistent in all other parables. In regard to the parable of the sower, in Mark 4:13 Jesus says that if they understand the symbolism of that parable, they can then rightly interpret all other parables.

And He said to them, "Do you not under-stand this parable? How then will you understand all the parables?"

Jesus did not change the symbolism from parable to parable. If a bird represented demons in one parable, it would represent demons in all other parables. This being true, Jesus said that the mustard seed growing into a mustard tree represented the kingdom of Heaven. It started small but became big. However, the larger it became, the more likely it was to become a lodging place for demons. This does not mean expressions of the kingdom of God are evil. It means that regardless of how pure we might try to keep something, the larger it becomes, the greater the propensity for devilish influence.

I watched this happen in the church I birthed and raised up. When everything was under my care and control it had a purity after God. The larger it became, the more I had to *trust* others with influence to guide and manage it. I later found that demonic things were happening in it. I was appalled at people I trusted, how selfish and self-propagating they were. I was astonished at the strife, compromise, and outright sin behind the scenes. Demons had gotten into the branches of what had, in its simplicity, been pure and after God's heart.

This is just a small example of how this can happen. Now multiply this within denominations, huge organizations, and ministries. There will be demonic influence that lodges in the branches of these organizations. When I give my money to these entities, depending on their level of demonic compromise, I can have claims against me from the demonic. My sacrifice of money connects me to these organizations. I may need to go before the Courts of Heaven and undo covenant claims the devil is making against me from past religious joining.

I have seen this to be true in those who were a part of the Catholic Church. This Church frequently partners with idolatry, so the devil can claim to own families who have their history in it. The same is true for Mormonism and other cultic offshoots of Christianity. We need to ask for judgments from the Courts of Heaven to undo covenantal rights being claimed against us.

This can be true even for mainstream denominations. I was in the Church of Christ prior to my family coming into the Spirit-filled life. I noticed that for decades I had limits on my prophetic abilities. Suddenly, after years in limited experience in the move of the Holy Spirit, it was revealed to me that the devil had a legal claim against me. Its roots were in my family's history in the Church of Christ. For decades we had been baptized into this church, which makes a covenant. We had given money and tithed on a regular basis, which is a sacrifice that makes a covenant.

The problem isn't that the Church of Christ is evil. However, they do not believe in the move of the Holy Spirit. They are very legalistic in their approach to the Word of God.

They believe only in the New Testament and not in the Old Testament as the Word of God. Demons had a right to restrict my prophetic encounters because of a covenantal bond in the spirit world with the Church of Christ. Once I went into the Courts of Heaven and repented and revoked any joining with this group, new encounters in the Holy Spirit began to occur. The curse was broken and limits were taken off.

In the next chapter there is an extensive prayer to help revoke demonic covenants that allow curses to land.

Chapter 5

REVOKING DEMONIC COVENANTS

Wherever there is a covenant made with demons in family history, these demons then claim these families for themselves. This happened in my life. I told you the story of how everything was falling to pieces in our lives. No amount of praying was changing anything. Instead, it was getting worse and worse. This is when the covenant with a demon god was uncovered. A seer saw clearly that someone in my bloodline had made a covenant with a demon god named Parax. I found out later that this demon god was known in history. It is defined as everything from a ruler of hell to a demon to a rebel. It also is associated with war and being a warrior. This thing was claiming the legal right to destroy me, claim my lineage, and do damage to my God-ordained purpose.

Someone in my ancestry had made a covenant with this thing. The Henderson lineage is from Scotland, and we were known for our fierceness and hostility in battle. Probably someone in my history had made a covenant with this demon god to be effective and win in warfare. I had to annul this. I had to go before the Courts of Heaven and ask for a judgment to revoke the claim this thing was making. Its claim was allowing the destruction of my family and my children's futures. When I stood in the Courts of Heaven and made my case, the legal rights of the demon were silenced. My family came free from the curse. How did I do this before the Courts?

First of all, I came and surrendered myself before the presence of the Lord. This is essential to operating in the Courts of Heaven and removing a curse's legal claims. Romans 12:1 tells us how important this is.

> I beseech you therefore, brethren, by the mercies of God, that you present your bodies a living sacrifice, holy, acceptable to God, which is your reasonable service.

The complete surrender of our entire being is the most logical thing we can do. In light of Jesus's great sacrifice for us, we must surrender and sacrifice ourselves to Him. James 4:7 also tells us that surrender is necessary to see the devil's rights revoked.

> Therefore submit to God. Resist the devil and he will flee from you.

When we submit ourselves to the Lord, power and authority to see the devil flee become ours. Our surrender to Jesus as the Lord of our life sets us in the right place to see the Courts act on our behalf.

The second thing I did was repent for any agreement with the demonic through my sin.

We are told in Psalm 32:5-6 that the godly are the ones who repent. So often people think it's the wicked and evil who need repentance. However, those who desire God with a passion are those who repent.

I acknowledged my sin to You, and my iniquity I have not hidden. I said, "I will confess my transgressions to the Lord," and You forgave the iniquity of my sin. Selah For this cause everyone who is godly shall pray to You in a time when You may be found; surely in a flood of great waters they shall not come near him.

The godly pray and repent to the Lord for any sin the devil could be using against us. When we do this, the blood of Jesus speaks on our behalf. It is the blood that removes the legal claims of the devil against us. When this is done, curses lose their right to function.

The third thing I did was repent for the covenant my ancestor had made with the demonic. Please realize that when I repent for the activities of my forefathers, I am not changing their eternal destiny. My repentance acknowledges the sin and revokes the legal claim of the devil to use that ancestral sin as a legal right against me. The blood of Jesus silences the claims of the devil based on the previous sin in my bloodline. Satan can no longer make claims against me from that covenant.

The fourth thing I did was give back anything the demonic could say I had gained from them. Remember that covenants with demons were made to gain some advantage—rain in season, power for war, protection from enemies, prosperity and wealth, and any number of other things. When we want out of the covenant with the demonic, they will claim we have gained things from them. We must be willing to give it back. We must be willing to pray and release anything from them that might have prospered us. We must simultaneously say that we want only what we have from the Lord and His blood that speaks for us. We know that all advantages actually come from His good hand. These statements must be made in the Courts of Heaven or the devil can contend that we shouldn't be allowed to go free.

The fifth thing I did was to renounce all association and agreement with the demonic. When I renounce something, I am declaring I will not have anything else to do with it. Second Corinthians 4:1-2 speaks of renouncing every hidden thing.

> *Therefore, since we have this ministry, as we have received mercy, we do not lose heart. But we have renounced the hidden things of shame, not walking in craftiness nor handling the word of God deceitfully, but by manifestation of the truth commending ourselves to every man's conscience in the sight of God.*

The word *renounce* is the Greek word *apeipomen* and means to "speak off oneself, to disown." Notice that not losing heart means renouncing hidden things. When we disown every agreement with demonic powers, a new strength and power will be ours. Every right to harass and sabotage our present and our future will be revoked and removed.

This is exactly what happened in my life. The ministry I had received was greatly empowered when the legal claims of curses were removed. We started living life on a whole new level because the restrictive effects of curses were revoked and annulled. Amazing new doors started to open. Finances began to increase. Influence began to grow. Probably the most amazing thing that happened was that my children began to come into divine order. They began to live out the future and destiny God had for them. I didn't know it at the time, but the covenant that was in my bloodline with the demonic allowed it to claim my lineage. When this was revoked and annulled, my children became free. They each began to pursue their God-ordained destiny with a passion. This was because the demonic ownership claimed over them was broken and they were set at liberty. Generational curses were revoked from our family line.

As I stand before Your Courts, Lord, I thank You for Your graciousness and favor. I come before You surrendering to You. I present myself as a living sacrifice in Your presence. May the words of my mouth and the meditations of my heart be acceptable before You. May I be submitted to You in every area that I might be judged by You as one who is Yours.

As I worship before You, Lord, I repent for any and all places of rebellion, disobedience, or unruliness. Forgive me for the places I have walked in disobedience to You. Cleanse me from my secret faults, redeem me from my presumptuous sins, and may I be innocent of the great transgression. May I be Your vessel walking in surrender and submission to You.

I also repent for any and all sins in my bloodline. Iniquity and all covenants with demons, known or unknown—may they be annulled by Your precious blood. I remind these Courts that I am purchased by the blood of Jesus that is speaking on my behalf. May this blood silence every claim against me. May every demonic assertion against me and my bloodline now be quiet. May every legal claim they make from covenants with demons in my bloodline no longer be able to speak. Their right to afflict me and my lineage is now revoked and removed in Jesus's name.

I also give back to these dark powers anything they claim I have gained from them. I want nothing that comes from them. I want no association on any level with them. I give back to them any and all things they claim to have given to me and my bloodline. I want only what belongs to me from the Lord. I want His blessings over me and my lineage. Every provision and blessing I enjoy, may it be from the Lord only.

I now renounce and speak off and disown any connection, agreement, or covenant with any idol, god, and demon power. I and my bloodline are now free from every hidden thing. They have no claim of ownership over me. I belong only to the Lord Jesus by His wonderful blood. Let every curse now be judged as illegal and unrighteous. It no longer has a right to land against me. I and my lineage are now free in Jesus's name, amen!

Chapter 6

CURSES CAUSED BY WORDS

A third cause that is used by the powers of darkness to land curses is *words*. Most would readily agree that words have power. In fact, Scripture is clear that there is life and death in the power of the tongue. We find this emphatic idea in Proverbs 18:21.

> *Death and life are in the power of the tongue, and those who love it will eat its fruit.*

I would have always consented to this concept from a theological and ideological standpoint. However, when I understood the Courts of Heaven, it made so much more sense. I became aware that Jesus has stripped the devil of his legal rights and claims. We must forcibly by faith set this in place to get the benefits. This is what we are actually doing in the Courts of Heaven. We are taking the legal work of Jesus and silencing the devilish powers that are seeking to hinder and destroy us with curses.

I have come to understand that people's words are used against us as testimony in the Courts of Heaven. In spite of what Jesus has done, words are sources for the devil to attack us in the Courts of Heaven. The devil can take our words and build cases with them against us. This is why many people are *cursed*. Someone of significance in their lives has spoken negative, death-producing words against them, or they have spoken them over their own life. If people with *positional authority* and/or *spiritual authority* have spoken negative reports about us, this can be very destructive. It allows the devil to make claims against us in the Courts of Heaven and see resulting curses land.

Let me give some scriptural references to help substantiate this idea. The first one is in

Numbers 13:31-33. It shows the ten spies who spied out the land of Canaan bringing an evil report. They had been commissioned by Moses to go look at the land. They were to gather intel that would help prepare the people to take the land. Instead, they came back with this faithless report of how big the enemy was.

> But the men who had gone up with him said, "We are not able to go up against the people, for they are stronger than we." And they gave the children of Israel a bad report of the land which they had spied out, saying, "The land through which we have gone as spies is a land that devours its inhabitants, and all the people whom we saw in it are men of great stature. There we saw the giants (the descendants of Anak came from the giants); and we were like grasshoppers in our own sight, and so we were in their sight."

Joshua and Caleb came back with a report of faith. They said they were well able to take the land. However, the other ten caused the hearts of the people to melt. Any faith they had to go take the land was disintegrated by the negative report. The result was a judgment of God from the Courts of Heaven. Remember that God is the Judge of all the earth. When they came back with *wrong words*, God rendered a verdict based on their wicked testimony. We find this verdict in Numbers 14:32-34.

> But as for you, your carcasses shall fall in this wilderness. And your sons shall be shepherds in the wilderness forty years, and bear the brunt of your infidelity, until your carcasses are consumed in the wilderness. According to the number of the days in which you spied out the land, forty days, for each day you shall bear your guilt one year, namely forty years, and you shall know My rejection.

God sentenced them to 40 years of wandering. For every day they searched and spied out the land, Israel as a nation would wander in the desert for a year. *The testimony, report, and words of ten men determined the destiny of a nation for 40 years!* Wow! This is the power of negative words. The whole nation was sentenced to 40 years of futility and aimless wandering because of the words of ten.

We must be so very careful of words of faithlessness and not believing God. We see this also in the life of a faithful man named Zacharias. Zacharias was a part of the priesthood and destined to be the father of John the Baptist. Yet when the angel showed up while Zacharias was performing his priestly function, Zacharias made a terrible mistake of questioning the angel. After the angel proclaimed the birth of John the Baptist to Zacharias and Elizabeth, his aged wife, Zacharias wanted to know *how* this could happen. The response of the angel is found in Luke 1:18-20.

> *And Zacharias said to the angel, "How shall I know this? For I am an old man, and my wife is well advanced in years."*

And the angel answered and said to him, "I am Gabriel, who stands in the presence of God, and was sent to speak to you and bring you these glad tidings. But behold, you will be mute and not able to speak until the day these things take place, because you did not believe my words which will be fulfilled in their own time."

The angel shut the mouth of Zacharias and made him unable to speak. He told him this was not just because he asked, "How could this be?" Remember that Mary asked the same question, and the angel who visited her patiently answered. However, Zacharias is said to have asked in unbelief. The angel knew that if Zacharias was able to speak for the next nine months, he would undo with his mouth what had been appointed by Heaven. The remedy was to shut his mouth and make him unable to speak.

Many times words abort the purposes of God. Our words can grant the devil a legal right to resist and withstand what God intends. We know that once John the Baptist was born, Zacharias's mouth opened again. When his words came into agreement with God's plan, he was allowed to speak and prophesy again. The word was that the baby to be born would be named John. The people were trying to abide by tradition and name him Zacharias, after his father. Zacharias was asked what his name should be. When he announced that it should be John as the angel had said, his mouth was opened. This is found in Luke 1:62-64.

> So they made signs to his father—what he would have him called.
>
> And he asked for a writing tablet, and wrote, saying, "His name is John." So they all marveled. Immediately his mouth was opened and his tongue loosed, and he spoke, praising God.

Zacharias had moved into faith. He could now be trusted to prophesy and declare the right things. If we want a voice that will influence, we must be a people who speak from the spirit of faith. We will be trusted with the purposes of God if we have this spirit of faith and speak the right things. However, if we are negative and cynical, our mouth and influence will be shut! Zacharias lost his voice until he moved into this dimension of faith. Once he transitioned into the faith realm, his voice was restored. This illustrates how significant and powerful our words are.

All words have significance. We are told this in 1 Corinthians 14:10.

There are, it may be, so many kinds of languages in the world, and none of them is without significance.

The word *languages* is the Greek word *phone*. It means "a tone, noise, sound, voice." Every voice has significance. Words have an impact and are used in the spirit world to create destiny. So no matter who speaks the words, there is some level of significance attached to them. However, when those who are in *positional authority* over your life or those who have *spiritual authority* in the spirit world speak, this can be devastating if these words are against you.

For instance, if your parents criticized you, the devil can take their words and build cases in the spirit world against you. This is what happened with my son Adam. He had made some wrong and bad choices. Nothing to warrant or cause what happened to him, however. Because of these choices and the choices of others, he found himself in deep depression. He felt that his life and future were over as far as God's purposes were concerned. One of the first times I went into the Courts of Heaven was on his behalf. Under the direction of the Spirit of the Lord, I repented for negative words I had spoken about him to his mother. I had *never* said negative things to him. But in my frustration with the circumstances, I had been critical of him in my speech to my wife. When I was standing in the Courts of Heaven, the Lord told me to repent for these words. He said, "The devil has taken your words against Adam and has said, 'Even his own father says this about him.'"

At this point I became aware that my position as Adam's father made my words much more powerful than I had considered. The devil was taking my words and using them to build a case against Adam. When I repented for my wrong words against Adam, God declared a judgment against the spirit of depression that was holding Adam. It had held him for over two years. In a matter of minutes, a two-plus-year bondage broke off Adam. He became free and began to move into his destiny and future! It was my words as his father that had been used against him.

Any words against us from those in *positional authority* should be dealt with aggressively in the Courts of Heaven. These words can give curses the right to land. This includes not only parents but also employers, church leadership, judges, civil leaders, and any others who occupy places of authority. They may not have an ounce of spiritual authority, but their position is used by the devil to build cases against us.

The other people whose words have tremendous weight in the spirit world are those with *spiritual authority*. This can be different from those with *positional authority*. Just because someone is in positional authority in and over our lives doesn't mean they carry spiritual authority. In fact, those with *spiritual authority* may not even be recognized in the natural world. However, they have tremendous power and authority in the unseen realm. Their call and life before God have granted them this place in the spirit dimension. When they speak, things move in the unseen world, resulting in things being reordered in the natural world.

The centurion recognized this about Jesus in Matthew 8:8-13. He didn't want Jesus to come into his house, even though Jesus was willing. This centurion realized that Jesus's spiritual authority only required Him to speak the word and things would be brought to divine order.

The centurion answered and said, "Lord, I am not worthy that You should come under my roof. But only speak a word, and my servant will be healed. For I also am a man under authority, having soldiers under me. And I say to this one, 'Go,' and he goes; and to another, 'Come,' and he comes; and to my servant, 'Do this,' and he does it."

When Jesus heard it, He marveled, and said to those who followed, "Assuredly, I say to you, I have not found such great faith, not even in Israel! And I say to you that many will come from east and west, and sit down with Abraham, Isaac, and Jacob in the kingdom of heaven. But the sons of the kingdom will be cast out into outer darkness. There will be weeping and gnashing of teeth." Then Jesus said to the centurion, "Go your way; and as you have believed, so let it be done for you." And his servant was healed that same hour.

Jesus spoke the word, and healing flowed into this centurion's home. The servant he loved was made whole because of the word of Jesus. This is a living picture of the power of any who carry spiritual authority. This is what can happen when right words are spoken by those with spiritual power in the unseen places.

However, if people with spiritual authority take up a cause against you, their words can have a devastating effect. It can grant the devil a case in the spirit world against you. I have had this happen to me. A very high-profile prophet decided they did not like me. For whatever reason, they had believed damning reports about me. They began to speak against me and bring criticisms against me. None of what they believed was true or correct. This didn't matter in the spirit world. The status they carried in the spirit world gave credibility to their words in the Courts of Heaven.

When I heard about what was being said, I laughed at it. I knew it wasn't true. However,

I did not then realize the principle I have just described. I erroneously thought that because it wasn't true, it could have no effect. The spiritual status of this prophet gave their words effect in the Courts of Heaven. Just as with my words as Adam's father, the devil took the words of this prophet and came before the Courts of Heaven against me. The devil's discourse was simply this: "Your prophet whom You have granted authority and status before You says this about Robert Henderson."

The prophet's status gave weight and power to the words that satan used to land a curse against me. Remember that I laughed at the report of this prophet when I heard it. The problem was that my life began to fall apart. I didn't realize that the words of someone with spiritual authority could grant satan a legal claim to land a curse. I needed to undo those words against me if I wanted the curse operating against me and my family to stop! Before I go into how to undo and annul words against us in the next chapter, let me establish *why* the words of those in a *position of authority* or with *spiritual authority* have such a negative effect.

In a natural court setting, when there is a trial there can be *expert witnesses* called to give testimony. These are people who are considered experts in a given field. The prosecution or the defense will call these witnesses. They are used to bolster or reinforce the claims being made in the court. They are meant to have a great impact because of their expertise in a specific field.

This is very similar to those with positional or spiritual authority in the unseen world. This is why the devil will take their words and make cases with them. They are already esteemed and have status in the Courts. Therefore, their words have an effect that others would not have. These words must definitely be undone and revoked. Otherwise, they can determine our lot and destiny. Curses will be allowed to land because of the case built by the devil on the basis of these words and testimonies.

Chapter 7

ANNULLING WORDS
THAT CAUSE CURSES

U ndoing and annulling words that
allow curses to land involves humility, repentance, forgiveness, and
statements and petitions made. Any time we
come before the Courts of Heaven, we must
come with a heart of humility. This is what is
accepted and received by the Lord. We are told
in 1 Peter 5:6 that humility will allow God to
exalt us in the proper time.

> *Therefore humble yourselves under the*
> *mighty hand of God, that He may exalt you*
> *in due time.*

If we desire to be effective in the Courts of Heaven, we must always approach this realm with humility and brokenness. We are told in Psalm 51:17 that a broken and contrite heart will not be rejected.

The sacrifices of God are a broken spirit, a broken and a contrite heart—These, O God, You will not despise.

"A broken and a contrite heart" means a heart that is yielded and submitted to the Lord. We are not justifying ourselves but allowing Him to be our justification. There have been several times in my life when there have been contentions with other people. They would accuse me of things I honestly did not feel I was guilty of. In spite of this, the Lord would require me to *take the blame and repent*. I didn't know why He was asking me to do this. But once I understood the Courts of Heaven, I began to understand. My willingness to become the culprit gave me status before His Court. I was letting Him be my justification and not justifying myself. This can have great power before the Lord. It allows Him to make right judgments on my behalf because I'm letting Him be my righteousness and justification.

The next step to undo words is a willingness to repent. Perhaps you are guilty of what you are being accused of, or at least partly to blame. Again, when I repent I am depending on His sacrifice to speak for me. We are told that we are to repent quickly in Matthew 5:25-26.

> Agree with your adversary quickly, while you are on the way with him, lest your adversary deliver you to the judge, the judge hand you over to the officer, and you be thrown into prison. Assuredly, I say to you, you will by no means get out of there till you have paid the last penny.

The word *adversary* is *antidikos* in the Greek. It means "an opponent in a lawsuit." In any case before us, we need to take the low road and repent. Otherwise, we can be handed over to the judge and go into a spiritual criminal justice system. However, if we will repent even when it seems we have nothing to repent for, we can be spared judgments. We have allowed the blood of Jesus to be our justification.

The next step is to make *statements under the direction of the Holy Spirit*. There are times when God will lead us to make statements before His Courts about unrighteous words against us that are untrue. I was facing delay. I was told opportunities were going to be set in place for me. However, these privileges lingered and were not manifesting. This had been a pattern in my life. When this happened, I got nervous. I went before the Courts of Heaven and asked, "Is there a case against me causing this delay?"

The truth is, I wasn't really expecting an answer, but instantly I heard the Lord say, "Yes, there is." He then told me I must come before His Courts and make the statement

Moses made when Korah was accusing him. This is found in Numbers 16:15.

> *Then Moses was very angry, and said to the Lord, "Do not respect their offering. I have not taken one donkey from them, nor have I hurt one of them."*

Korah's accusations continued after Moses had sought to appeal and reason with him. Moses then made this statement. When I heard the Lord tell me to make this same statement, I knew others were accusing me of taking something that wasn't mine. I needed to silence the words that were letting a curse of delay operate. I had an awareness that this statement would allow the Lord to search out the records of Heaven. He would see if my statement was correct. If it was found to be correct, the Lord could render a judgment against the words spoken against me.

Obviously, God is all-knowing and knew that the words were untrue. However, for legal operations He needed me to make the case that would undo these words and free me from the curse of delay. This is exactly what happened. Within two days the delay ended and what had been promised manifested. It led to great blessings and privileges to this very day. In other words, it set things in motion that allowed the word concerning the Courts of Heaven to touch the nations!

Another step is to forgive. If I am to get free from words that are allowing curses, I must forgive those who spoke them. Any bitterness and anger toward those who spoke those words can hold me in the curse. We are clearly told in Matthew 6:14-15 that we must forgive to be forgiven.

For if you forgive men their trespasses, your heavenly Father will also forgive you. But if you do not forgive men their trespasses, neither will your Father forgive your trespasses.

I cannot ask for words against me to be forgiven if I don't forgive those who spoke against me. We must embrace the same grace that has forgiven us to be able to forgive others. My anger and ill will toward others will forbid the forgiveness I need to be free from curses. As we forgive, we are freeing the Courts of Heaven to render good and right decisions on our behalf. Curses caused by words against us will be revoked and removed.

The last thing we should do to undo curses caused by words is petition the Courts. We should ask for every word that has been speaking against us in the Courts of Heaven to be annulled. We should ask that it be blotted out and not allowed any place before God to speak. Anything that has claimed a right to speak against us would be silenced and not allowed to speak. There are two scriptures I use to petition the Courts for any and every word to be abolished. One is Romans 3:4, which declares that only God is true.

Certainly not! Indeed, let God be true but every man a liar. As it is written: "That You may be justified in Your words, and may overcome when You are judged."

In other words, God's verdict as Judge over-comes the words and opinions of all others. God is true. I make this statement and declare that on this basis the words of men be silenced. The other scripture is Zechariah 2:13.

Be silent, all flesh, before the Lord, for He is aroused from His holy habitation!

When the Lord rises in judgment, all flesh is made to be silent. Every word is brought to silence. The words against us are now silenced and curses they have caused are revoked and undone.

Lord, as I come before Your Courts, I present my case that every word against me may be silenced. I submit myself in humility. I acknowledge that You are the great God and my times are held in Your hand. I ask that You might exalt me in due time. I declare that You alone are my righteousness and justification.

I also approach Your Courts and repent. I ask that I might be forgiven for anything that has allowed a word to be spoken against me. I acknowledge any place where I have sinned and therefore words are being spoken against me. I ask that Your precious blood would speak for me. I am sorry for any place this is allowing curses to work.

I also listen to the Holy Spirit as my legal aid. Anywhere I need to make statements that set in motion Your legal system on my behalf, I obey and agree. Let that which is for me in Your Courts work on my behalf.

I also forgive those who have spoken against me. I acknowledge that without Your grace, I am guilty of the same thing. I forgive them for speaking words that have allowed satan to land curses. I ask, Lord, that You might forgive them and forgive me.

I also ask that my petition for the silencing and annulling of these words would now be heard. Let every word that is allowing curses to land now be revoked and quieted. May they no longer be heard in Your Courts as testimony against me. In Jesus's name, let these words be dismissed and no longer valid before You as my Judge. In Jesus's name, amen.

Chapter 8

SILENCING VOICES

There are voices resonating in the spirit world. These voices are so often the accuser speaking against us. These voices cause curses to work against us. If we are to see curses revoked, we must first see these spiritual voices silenced. Understanding this requires insight from two scriptures. The first one is Isaiah 54:17. This scripture gives us revelation about the activity in the unseen world.

"No weapon formed against you shall prosper, and every tongue which rises against you in judgment you shall condemn. This is the heritage of the servants of the Lord, and their righteousness is from Me," says the Lord.

Notice that weapons will not prosper or be successful because the *tongues* against us are condemned. In other words, it's the *tongues* that are speaking against us that cause the weapons/curses to land. If we can silence the tongues, the weapons will not have any power.

When I began to practice this principle, my effectiveness in the Courts of Heaven sky-rocketed. Instead of going after the weapons, I went after the tongues, which I clearly have the right to condemn. This is all from a legal perspective. The word *judgment* is the Hebrew word *misphat*. It means "a judicial verdict." We are being told that we can come before the Courts of Heaven and see tongues be con-demned when they are claiming a legal right to land curses. They are themselves judged as illegal and unrighteous before the Lord and made to be silent!

The word *condemn* in the Hebrew means "to declare as wrong." Notice that I have the right to do this for two reasons. Or we could say two things are giving me status in the

Courts of Heaven to revoke these tongues. The first is that I have a heritage and inheritance as the servant of the Lord. This is my legal right as the servant of the Lord. When I serve Him with my whole heart, I can stand in the Courts of Heaven and see judgments against demonic tongues that desire to land curses. The second thing that grants status in the Courts of Heaven is His righteousness. This prophetically means that all Jesus did to make us the *righteousness of God in Christ Jesus* allows us to stand in His Courts. In other words, I have a right to stand in the Courts because of His righteousness on my behalf. From this position, I am able to silence the tongues.

Instead of going after the weapon or curse, legally go after the tongue. Once the tongue driving the weapon is revoked and annulled, the weapon will not be able to operate. The voices in the spirit world must be silenced. We see how to do this effectively in Revelation 12:10-11.

Then I heard a loud voice saying in heaven, "Now salvation, and strength, and the kingdom of our God, and the power of His Christ have come, for the accuser of our brethren, who accused them before our God day and night, has been cast down. And they overcame him by the blood of the Lamb and by the word of their testimony, and they did not love their lives to the death."

Here we see the accuser of the brothers bringing claims against the people of God. This is all legal. The word *accuser* is the Greek word *kategoros*. It means "a complainant at law." In other words, an *accuser* is one bringing a legal accusation. This is what the devil and his forces are. They bring legal action against us as the saints of God. These accusations are requesting and requiring the right to land curses. Notice that the accuser's words are against us day and night. In other words, there is a steady stream of legal reasons being given to harass and curse us as the people of God. We must come before the

Courts of Heaven and silence the voices of these accusers. Remember, it is the voice and the tongue that create and drive the weapons and curses.

We are told three things to do to overcome the accuser bringing legal proceedings against us. One, we use the blood of the Lamb. We will deal more with this in the final chapter. It is the blood that gives us legal status as the righteousness of God. It is the blood that declares we are New Testament believers. We must come before the Courts and let the blood of the Lamb speak for us. His blood will dismiss all cases against us. Through repentance, we come into agreement with the blood of the Lamb. First John 1:7 tells us that if we walk in the light, which is repentance, His blood works for us.

But if we walk in the light as He is in the light, we have fellowship with one another, and the blood of Jesus Christ His Son cleanses us from all sin.

When we walk in the light, that means we are being honest and repenting for sins and faults. This lets us fellowship with Jesus and the saints. It also causes the blood of Jesus to *keep on* cleansing us from all sin. This is the verbiage in the Greek. It's not something that cleanses us once, but it perpetually cleanses us from every sin and fault. This revokes the devil's legal claim against us to land curses. We ask for the blood to speak for us and agree with its testimony before the Courts of Heaven. This allows the decision to be rendered that whatever accusation is being presented is illegal and unrighteous because of the blood!

We also overcome the accuser's voice demanding the right to land curses through the *word of our testimony*. Whereas the blood of the Lamb dismisses cases against us, the word of our testimony presents cases for us. We must learn how to make our case before the Courts of Heaven. This is primarily done by calling God into remembrance of what He has said about us. Isaiah 43:26 is clear with this. God is a covenant keeping God and loves when we use His word to create cases for His purposes in and through us.

> Put Me in remembrance; let us contend together; state your case, that you may be acquitted.

Notice that putting God in remembrance is *contending* in a legal sense. This word in Hebrew is *shaphat*. It means to litigate. It means to *judge*. The Lord is encouraging us to make our case together with His help. Remember that the Holy Spirit is the One who is our legal aid. He will help us litigate before the Lord so that curses are revoked and futures are secured. This is how we state our case and see judgments rendered and ourselves acquitted. Every legal cause against us is revoked!

The last thing is that we silence voices in the spirit world through having a status before the Courts. Not only do we use the blood of the Lamb to dismiss cases and the word of our testimony to present cases, but we also love not our lives unto death. This deals with our choice to do His will rather than our own. As we lay down our lives for His Word and cause, this grants us status in the Courts from which we can present our case more effectively. The more we say yes to the Lord and no to our flesh, the more authority we are granted before Him. This allows us to stand in the Courts and ask that any and every voice against us be silenced and revoked. Their legal claim to land curses is removed from our lives. When curses come off, everything changes.

Lord, as I come before Your Courts, I ask that every voice demanding the right to curse me and my generations be revoked. I remind this Court that I am Your servant. This is my heritage. It is my right as Your vessel to see these voices condemned and judged as illegal and unrighteous. I am also the righteousness of God because of the blood of the Lamb. Therefore, let it be known that I have the right to stand here in this place and request and require this of this Court.

I ask that all voices of accusers against me be silenced. I call this Court into remembrance that the blood of Jesus has purchased me. I do not have any connection to the demonic. I belong to Jesus because of His blood. Every other claim of ownership and right to land curses against me is revoked. Your blood has redeemed me from every curse. Let Your Holy Spirit now set in place all that the blood has done.

I also bring my case before You through the word of my testimony. Let it be known that I call God into remembrance of all that You have said. I remind this Court that my God is a covenant keeping God. All that He has promised and all that He has declared, let it come to pass. Let every curse that would resist the covenant promises of

God be annulled. Let it be found to be illegal and unrighteous before this Court. Let the word and promise of God be seen fully in my life.

I also declare before this Court that I lay my life down before You. I love not my life unto death. I declare that You, Lord, and Your purposes are the greatest thing in my life. Thank You that You empower me and give me grace to say yes to You and no to my flesh. I choose You over everything else. May this grant me a place of authority and status before Your Courts. Let every curse that would resist Your divine will in me and my generations lose its right to operate. Let every voice claiming its right to function now be declared unrighteous and illegal in Jesus's name, amen!

Chapter 9

THE BLOOD THAT SPEAKS

The ability to revoke the rights of curses in the Courts of Heaven is accomplished through the blood of Jesus. The legality of the blood of Jesus is everything we need to annul the voices and see curses revoked. One of the main things I do is use and agree with the speaking blood of Jesus. Hebrews 12:24 is a very important scripture. It speaks of the blood of sprinkling and its voice on our behalf.

To Jesus the Mediator of the new covenant, and to the blood of sprinkling that speaks better things than that of Abel.

This scripture, taken in context, is revealing the spiritual dimension we have been granted access to. If we were to read from verse 22 on, we would find that we have been given entrance into a legal place of much activity on our behalf. Among the things working and moving for us is the *blood of sprinkling that is speaking.* It actually says it is speaking better things than that of Abel. Remember that Cain, Abel's brother, killed him in a fit of jealousy and envy. Abel's offering was accepted by the Lord while Cain's was rejected. The result was that Abel's blood cried out for judgment and justice against Cain. We find God confronting Cain in Genesis 4:8-12 because of what Abel's blood was legally stating before Him.

> *Now Cain talked with Abel his brother; and it came to pass, when they were in the field, that Cain rose up against Abel his brother and killed him.*
>
> *Then the Lord said to Cain, "Where is Abel your brother?"*
>
> *He said, "I do not know. Am I my brother's keeper?"*

And He said, "What have you done? The voice of your brother's blood cries out to Me from the ground. So now you are cursed from the earth, which has opened its mouth to receive your brother's blood from your hand. When you till the ground, it shall no longer yield its strength to you. A fugitive and a vagabond you shall be on the earth."

Notice that the vengeance required by the voice of Abel's blood caused God to judge Cain severely. He was sentenced to being a vagabond and fugitive. He was sentenced to live out his life in futility. He was sentenced to no prosperity. This judgment was a result of the testimony of Abel's blood. This was a curse set on Cain. However, we are told that the blood of sprinkling now speaking for us is speaking better things than that of Abel. The blood of Jesus is crying for forgiveness, redemption, restoration, and renewal. Jesus's blood is granting God the legal right He needs to forgive. God's heart was always to forgive. Jesus's blood now grants Him the right to do this.

There are three things we should know about Jesus's blood. First of all it is *sprinkled*. This is significant. The blood of Jesus is sprinkled in two locations. It is sprinkled on the mercy seat of Heaven in the Holiest of Holies. It is also sprinkled in our hearts. After Jesus died on the cross, He then ascended to Heaven. He took His own blood and applied it to the real altar in Heaven. Revelation 11:19 shows the temple of God in Heaven being opened and the ark of the covenant in that temple.

> *Then the temple of God was opened in heaven, and the ark of His covenant was seen in His temple. And there were lightnings, noises, thunderings, an earthquake, and great hail.*

The ark and the tabernacle Moses assembled were replicas of the ones he saw in Heaven. When Jesus died on the cross, He took His own blood and sprinkled it and poured it out in this temple. From this location in Heaven, His blood is speaking for the salvation of all humankind. This is why when someone cries out, they will be saved. We are told in Romans 10:13 that *whoever* cries for salvation will have it.

For *"whoever calls on the name of the Lord shall be saved."*

This is because of the speaking blood that is crying out from the authentic temple in Heaven. Jesus has deposited His blood there. Hebrews 9:24-26 shows us Jesus taking His own blood into this holy place in Heaven.

For Christ has not entered the holy places made with hands, which are copies of the true, but into heaven itself, now to appear in the presence of God for us; not that He should offer Himself often, as the high priest enters the Most Holy Place every year with blood of another—He then would have had to suffer often since the foundation of the world; but now, once at the end of the ages, He has appeared to put away sin by the sacrifice of Himself.

Jesus entered into Heaven itself and appeared in the presence of God for us all. He only needed to take His blood into that holy place once. It is there now, speaking for us, to bring us into the full salvation that is ours. All curses can be revoked and removed because of the voice of this blood.

The blood of sprinkling is also speaking in our hearts. Hebrews 10:22 lets us know that our consciences are renewed. They are restored to a place of innocence. They are no longer filled with voices condemning us. They are filled with a sense of acceptance and approval from God.

Let us draw near with a true heart in full assurance of faith, having our hearts sprinkled from an evil conscience and our bodies washed with pure water.

No longer will a defiled, evil conscience that testifies against us keep us away from God. We are now able to come before Him in full faith because of a conscience that has been sprinkled with and redeemed by the blood. So many people struggle with acceptance before God. This in itself is a curse. The voice of the sprinkled blood in our hearts will confirm us and affirm us before the Lord. This is because there is no longer blood crying for our judgment. The blood of sprinkling is now crying for redemption.

A second thing we should know about the blood of sprinkling is that it *is speaking*, not just that it *has spoken*. If the blood had only spoken, it would have taken care of only our past sins. However, since it is speaking, it also redeems us from our present and even future sins. The speaking blood is so powerful that it brings us legally into full salvation. Remember that the Holy Spirit functionally brings us into all that the blood has done. This means we have to walk in surrender to the Spirit to get the full redemption. If I rebel, the Spirit cannot bring me into the fullness the blood is crying for. We must walk in submission and surrender to the Holy Spirit in our lives. There is provision for every sin we will ever commit, but we must surrender our lives in a lifestyle of repentance to Jesus through the Holy Spirit. This is the only practical way curses can be removed from our lives.

The third thing about the sprinkled blood is that we have *come to it*. This is the whole essence of this portion of Scripture. We have been repositioned in the spirit world to get the benefit of the sprinkled blood. We must simply access and embrace by faith all that Jesus has done. It's there for us. It's available. Reach out and get it and watch the legal rights of curses be revoked. The Holy Spirit will move, and all that has been harassing and limiting will be gone forever. There is freedom in all that Jesus has done for us. Appeal to the Courts of Heaven and experience the goodness of the Lord.

As I come before Your Courts, Lord,
I thank You for Your speaking blood.
Thank You so much for Your sacrifice

that allows the blood to speak for me and my generations. Thank You that Your blood is sprinkled in Heaven and grants God the legal right to forgive and redeem. Thank You that Your blood is sprinkled in my heart and redeems my defiled conscience. I ask before Your Courts that all Your blood legally did would now be mine through the power of and encounter with Your Holy Spirit.

Thank You, Lord, that Your blood is speaking for me and my generations. Lord, You are a covenant keeping God. Thank You that everything legally necessary for past sins, present sins, and future sins has been provided by the blood. Let every legal claim of the devil know that any right to afflict with a curse is removed by the testimony of Your blood and the power of the Holy Spirit.

I also thank You, Lord, that I have been repositioned in the spirit world. I am not trying to get somewhere; I am set there already by You and what You have done. I have already come to the blood of sprinkling that redeems me from every curse. I am free. The legal claims of the devil against me are revoked and removed. I stand in Your Courts and receive all You have provided for me. Let every curse be removed and let me and my generations go free. In Jesus's name, amen!

ABOUT
ROBERT HENDERSON

Robert Henderson is a global apostolic leader who operates in revelation and impartation. His teaching empowers the body of Christ to see the hidden truths of Scripture clearly and apply them for breakthrough results. Driven by a mandate to disciple nations through writing and speaking, Robert travels extensively around the globe, teaching on the apostolic, the kingdom of God, the Seven Mountains, and most notably the Courts of Heaven. He has been married to Mary for 40 years. They have six children and five grandchildren. Together they are enjoying life in beautiful Waco, Texas.

YOUR Prophetic COMMUNITY

Are you passionate about hearing God's voice, walking with Jesus, and experiencing the power of the Holy Spirit?

Destiny Image is a community of believers with a passion for equipping and encouraging you to live the prophetic, supernatural life you were created for!

We offer a fresh helping of practical articles, dynamic podcasts, and powerful videos from respected, Spirit-empowered, Christian leaders to fuel the holy fire within you.

Sign up now to get awesome content delivered to your inbox
destinyimage.com/sign-up

 Destiny Image